BETTER SPORT BRIGHTER FUTURE

Utilising sport to develop character, self-confidence and overall wellbeing in primary students

David & Leanne Telfer

Published 2020

Million Dollar Author

Copyright © 2020 by David & Leanne Telfer

All rights reserved. No part of this publication may be reproduced, distributed or transmitted in any form or by any means, without prior written permission.

Million Dollar Author publishing
Sydney, Australia

Book Layout © 2020 Million Dollar Author

Better Sport, Brighter Future. -- 1st ed.
ISBN 978-0-9943007-7-5

Dedication

We are both so thankful to the people in our lives who have impacted and shaped who we are through sport and their often thankless commitment to endless training sessions and competitions. These people constantly encouraged us to be fearless in our quest to achieve, often beyond what we thought we could. It was not until we had our own kids that we realised the bigger picture they had. It was not simply about getting a gold medal but about the person that is being shaped and strengthened through the highs and lows, the wins and losses, making teams and not making teams, the tears and the cheers, and the strong ties and connections. This will stay with us for life.

We are so thankful that they understood a bigger picture and gave us the opportunity to have sport ingrained in us for life. To be now able to be a part of that process for others, and have the opportunity to impact them through sport, is a privilege and tremendously rewarding.

ABOUT THE AUTHORS

David and Leanne Telfer founded *Be Skilled Be Fit* in 2000 with a passion to not only develop the sporting skills of the students they teach, but to assist those students' overall social, emotional, mental, and behavioural strength through sport.

As sports providers we see that we have the perfect opportunity to team with teachers and shape students so they're ready to thrive.

What Australian sports pros and schools have to say about working with David, Leanne and the *Be Skilled Be Fit* team:

My involvement in sport has had a huge impact on my life. I have been able to make lifelong friends through my involvement in many different sports and many of the friendships I formed through sport, some from when I was ten years old, still stand today. Sport taught me how to work together as a member of a team, to be a leader, and to have fun whilst still giving it my absolute best.

A lot of the basic physical skills I developed as a child was through my involvement in many sports: athletics, basketball, gymnastics, and swimming, to name a few. I loved being involved and having a go with my friends. It was through trying many different sports that I realised I loved throwing discus more than anything; this passion has led me to where I am today. I still love throwing like I did when I was ten, and it has given me so much more in return. Get out there and give everything a go! You never know what you might have a passion for.

It is understanding these principles and how important it is in having "sport done right" that has seen me partner ***Be Skilled Be Fit*** with their

Special Event Sports Days over the past eight years.

Dani Stevens
Australian World Champion discus thrower,
Competed at three Olympic and three Commonwealth Games

Wheeler Heights Public School is so thankful to have found ***Be Skilled Be Fit***. We have been utilising the gymnastics and athletics programs for a number of years and cannot fault the professionalism of all involved. The staff taking the students for their activities are knowledgeable, caring, and friendly, and engage the students thoroughly. The programs have been differentiated to ensure talented students were extended whilst those requiring assistance were given modified programs and additional support. Due to this, our students have shown extensive growth in their abilities in these areas and all students have been able to achieve success. David is always accommodating and flexible with any requests made and ensures that BSBF are a pleasure to deal with. We would recommend BSBF to any school!

Priscilla Wright
Assistant Principal, Instructional Leader
Wheeler Heights Public School

It has been an absolute joy working with ***Be Skilled Be Fit***. The team has been fantastic! The ease of booking, timetabling, all the way through to the staff who were engaged in teaching the children were all first class. The students have been actively engaged, and encouraged, and achieved Personal Bests whilst enjoying the athletics program. The last few years, our school's athletics results have been poor with many children unable to make qualifying distances and/or heights. With the assistance of expert, explicit instruction, this year we have numerous children reaching qualifying distances/heights in every age group! The students themselves have thoroughly enjoyed participating in this weekly program as it not only gets them out of the classroom but helps them actively participate in our school's athletics carnival. From a whole staff point of view, I have only heard rave reviews about the manner, rapport, and studious nature of the staff providing lessons for our students. We are certainly very glad we have taken the first step in turning around our school's athletics results and look forward to working with BSBF in the future. They are definitely a standard above the rest.

David Reid
Assistant Principal
Glenhaven Public School

We are so pleased that you are coming here next term; there is no one better.

Principal
Western Sydney Public School

Our school employed ***Be Skilled Be Fit*** to run our K-2 gymnastics and 3-6 athletics programs across our large school. David, Daniel, and their team were at all times accommodating of our complex timetable and limited spaces. The program itself was very professionally run and thoroughly assessed. All equipment was provided and of a high quality.

The BSBF staff taught the specific skills required for our Athletics Carnival, then spent additional time 'shortlisting' for our Field Events. This made our school Athletics Carnival much easier to run for us as a school of close to 1,000 students.

Our K-2 students loved attending gymnastics each week and received specific feedback about how to improve. Teachers and parents have reported just how impressed they are with the program. So much so that we have engaged BSBF to run our 3-6 gymnastics program this term.

Deputy Principal
Western Sydney Public School

The team at ***Be Skilled Be Fit*** was fantastic; they had easy to follow methods and explanations to teach the kids skills and fun activities to build up their skills in each task. The team had great behaviour management of my class and kept all of the kids engaged and participating. "The instructors were very nice and very helpful" (I asked the kids).

My students loved the program and left every lesson so proud of what they were able to accomplish.

Some of the differences are that the kids are supportive of each other and encourage one another to do their best. After understanding and realising how hard some new skills can be they have become more understanding of different ability levels and more supportive of one another.
Teacher
Glenhaven Public School

Our students' parents are very protective of what you are doing; you are part of the culture here and highly valued.
Principal
Sydney School

Be Skilled Be Fit has conducted our school's gym/PE program over six years. During this time the quality of their programs, and of the BSBF staff who run them, has been consistently outstanding. All of the children at our school – even those who would not normally be considered sporty – look forward to their weekly lesson with BSBF.

As one of our school's Primary Schools Sports Association (PSSA) sports coaches, I have seen a massive change during the time BSBF have been with us. Indeed, I consider that 'transformation' is not too strong a word for the change in the skills and, probably just as importantly, the attitude of our students towards sport. We have gone from being a 'non-sporty' school to being a very sporty school. Our PSSA teams have gone from consistently placing near the bottom of competitions, to placing (as they do now) consistently at or very near to the top. That's in all PSSA sports across boys and girls!

There is no doubt in my mind that BSBF's involvement with our school has been the major contributor to this turnaround.

BSBF are thorough professionals, great people to deal with – flexible, considerate, always willing to fit in with the needs of the school – and loved by our students. We could not ask for more!
Kel Cowling
Teacher/Librarian and PSSA Coach,
Seaforth Public School

CONTENTS

WHY SPORT IS SO IMPORTANT TO CHILDREN'S DEVELOPMENT	1
THE EFFECTS OF SPORT DONE POORLY	8
WINNING IS ABOUT MORE THAN MEDALS	17
FEAR OF FAILURE	27
ACKNOWLEDGEMENT AND ATTENTION	38
ENGAGEMENT AND CONNECTIVITY	45
WHAT TO LOOK FOR IN YOUR SPORTS PROVIDER	61
OUR STORY	68
HOW TO CONTACT US	73

CHAPTER ONE

WHY SPORT IS SO IMPORTANT TO CHILDREN'S DEVELOPMENT

Why is sport, when taught correctly, such a profound positive influence on children's development?

The sporting platform helps address the emotional development of children and when implemented correctly, can go hand in hand with classroom teaching.

Why is it so effective? It's a fun and engaging platform. You're outside in a different environment, you're not sitting in the classroom, and students feel like it's 'playtime'. It's sporty professional people engaging positively with students in their sports lesson, and this allows you to get the best out of them in that environment.

The sport environment evokes many mental, emotional and social situations that children have to deal with constantly. Sport classes done well are another classroom, incorporating both sports skills and life skills, that can really enhance the actual classroom experience for children and teachers alike.

We are finding that there is a major disconnect between the opportunities that are available for students and the willingness of students to engage and thrive within those opportunities.

This situation can be frustrating and problematic for teachers who can see much greater potential in this generation.

As educators we need to be asking ourselves the question: "why is there resistance from the students toward reaching their potential ?"

As we can all probably agree, a major area where some children are currently being let down is the development of life skills. A lack of life skills, including social skills is leading to issues surrounding poor mental health.[1]

Three key areas that we are seeing consistently in the students we teach are:

1. Fear of failure
2. Need for acknowledgement and attention
3. Lack of engagement and connection

This generation is experiencing life differently to previous generations due to the abundance of what is readily available to them. They have access to so much and from such a young age, when their development is not ready for it.

There are great things about what is available to them but also many pitfalls surrounding it. They have access to technology and information at a greater level than any generation previous, but at the same time they're not developing the emotional maturity and life skills to be able to handle that.

---

[1] Blue, A. (6 November 2017). Poor social skills may be harmful to mental and physical health. The University of Arizona. https://uanews.arizona.edu.

Previously, our emotional, behavioural and psycological maturity used to grow along side the growth of interlect. Now, not only is their intellectual education accelerated, but children are being exposed to material largely during online screen time that they do not have the emotional maturity to manage. Ironically studies have shown that than too much online screen time is associated with lower psychological wellbeing and less emotional stability.[2]

While schools are focused on learning outcomes and academic achievement, the opportunity exists for schools to utilise the sport platform as a mechanism to develop students not only physically but socially, mentally, and emotionally. This will aid and support what teachers are already doing in the classroom by further shaping and developing their life skills.

As school sports providers, we are fortunate to be the 'fun' in a student's day. The students approach it with a different attitude because it doesn't feel like 'work'. Students don't even

---

[2] Campbell, W. K. and Twenge, J. M. (18 October 2018). Associations between screen time and lower psychological well-being among children and adolescents: Evidence from a population-based study. Preventative Medicine Reports, 271–283. 10.1016/j.pmedr.2018.10.003.

realise that they are being shaped mentally, emotionally, and socially because it happens naturally as part of sport, provided they have positive, strong sports educators guiding them.

It's also an environment of play, which studies show is important to not only a child's development but continuing through whole of life. - though modern children aren't doing as much of it as in previous generations.[34]

For many children, life has become highly pressured. There is so much pressure put on children emotionally across many areas of their lives. The challenge for the grown-ups in their lives is to unpack where that pressure is coming from, why that pressure is there and why they are not managing that pressure in a healthy or productive way.

If we can bring fun and play back into their day, if we can keep sports, gymnastics, athletics, and PE engaging, playful and fun, then we have an opportunity to address the things such as 'fear of

---

[3] Robinson, L, Smith, M M.A., Segal, J Ph.D, Shubin, J. (June 2019). The Benefits of Play for Adults. www.helpguide.org/articles/mental-health/benefits-of-play-for-adults.html.

[4] Entin, E. (12 October 2011). All Work and No Play: why your kids are more anxious, depressed . The Atlantic. www.theatlantic.com/health/archive/2011/10/all-work-and-no-play-why-your-kids-are-more-anxious-depressed/246422/.

failure', 'acknowledgement and attention', and 'engagement and connection'.

For some people, play may seem like a frivolous activity to simply give students a break between lessons, but it is probably one of the most crucial elements in developing problem-solving, leadership, creativity, imagination, teamwork, self-exploration, self-management, and socialisation skills.

We have seen how play impacts the way students interact with their classmates, teammates, peers, family and, ultimately, their work colleagues.

Being sports providers, we are in a great position because we get to do the 'play'; we get to be the fun part of a student's day. In fact, in our business, one of our core values is that our staff need to understand that we are a really fun part of the day. Remember when your parents used to ask, "What was your favourite part of the day?" Of course, the answer would often be "lunch time" - because you got to play.

We love that we get to provide students with structured fun in their day. Even better, they are getting 'adult attention' in their play, which children thrive on. It is always our hope that we provide a happy, structured part of their day that transfers into productive learning in the classroom.

We acknowledge that play has to be purposeful; it is important that school sports are not just unrestricted play. Our lessons are highly structured and planned to meet all learning outcomes.

It is our intention to work with teachers to create a greater learning experience across the Personal Development Health & Physical Education (PDHPE) curriculum, highlighted by greater personal growth and skill development for the students.

At its best, when sport is done right, it's about much more than play and fun. It's about integrating life skills into children's lives, often without them even realising it. At *Be Skilled, Be Fit* we are committed to doing sport right and maximising those broad outcomes for our students, teachers and schools.

CHAPTER TWO

THE EFFECTS OF SPORT DONE POORLY

In life, we are always learning, either intentionally or unintentionally. Whether you are intentionally teaching something, intentionally learning something, or whether it's unintentional, it's constantly happening. Unless you are intentional about what you want children to learn, then potentially they will learn the wrong thing.

For example, we may be attending a luncheon, a party, a wedding, or it could be a sports training session with our kids. If we arrive late then we are demonstrating to our kids that lateness is okay.

They have learnt that people who are waiting for them don't matter, they have learnt disrespect for others, and they have learnt poor time management. This is a short list of many things that can be learnt from one small thing.

Unless you have an intentional plan for learning, children will learn 'unintentionally'. Children are sponges, taking in everything that is going on around them. If adults model poor habits or destructive behaviours, then that is what children will learn.

Sport is such a great vehicle for development; we don't want any child to miss out on the positive opportunities it presents. However, if we don't do it right then children won't get the right message. This is not just relevant to the actual sports skills they will learn, like throwing, catching, and kicking, it extends to the mental, emotional, and behavioural learning that happens in sport as well.

If they're learning great life skills like resilience, how to manage their own behaviour to support their teammates, how to develop their skills and receive feedback so that they can excel, then that is a positive experience.

However, not everybody gets that positive experience of sport. We probably see more people saying, "Actually, I had a coach or a teacher that told me I was no good at this as a kid." Those kinds of comments have had a negative effect on many people.

There are so many ways we can fail our children on the sporting platform.

- ❖ Their sports teacher may model a bad attitude toward sport.
- ❖ They may not have good sportsmanship demonstrated.
- ❖ They may not be encouraged to always put in effort.
- ❖ They may not be shown how to recognise their own small wins.
- ❖ They may not be encouraged to strive to improve.
- ❖ They may not be coached to be okay with their 'losses'.
- ❖ They may not be encouraged to get out of their comfort zone.

This list is endless, in fact we could write an entire book on the effects of sport coached poorly.

Further to that, which is the scary bit, you don't even have to be overly 'bad' or destructive to have a negative impact on a student. Even simply saying, "Well, don't worry the bell will go soon," might prevent a child from having their own win or small achievement in that lesson. Instead it gives the child the message that they are not good at it, but that's okay, it's just sport.

Another example might be when a student can't throw a ball into the bucket in front of their peers. The child's feelings of failure, embarrassment and shame, which if unrecognised and unresolved, can translate into anxiety and behavioural problems. Such a small thing can become such a major thing for children if not addressed properly and promptly.

Naturally, the aim is to always be as positive as possible. However, as nice as it is to say "good try", this doesn't help them to do it correctly the next time and we are still setting them up to fail.

If a student has a problem with a maths question, you would look at where they went wrong and offer strategies to improve. It is exactly the same for sport. By giving continual, constructive, and positive feedback children can make improvements by altering technique. By doing this, their success rate immediately improves and that can completely alter the course of their next emotional, mental, and behavioural responses.

This feedback slowly helps students to be comfortable with not having immediate success all the time, and seeing that challenges are what propel us to new success if we are willing to take small risks. For example, the risk of possibly 'failing' in front of our peers at first.

On the flip side, if the child doesn't get supported, coached or mentored properly, not only do they have immediate failure, their mental, emotional, and behavioural state changes for the worse.

The emotional response to 'failure' can look different depending on the child. Using the example above, on the next throw the student might decide to throw it as silly as he can, or maybe as far away as he can, to see if he can get a laugh from his peers. He would prefer them to laugh at his intentional silliness than feel like they are laughing at him for not being able to throw a ball in a bucket. Now with this silliness he finds himself in trouble and having to sit out of sport. This then leads to a negative mindset that he will take into the classroom or the playground, where he finds himself in trouble for something else. This leads to a detention, then being in trouble at home. From a seemingly small thing, which can be easily altered, we see a sudden spiral out of control. When a child's emotional state is fragile their mental state tries to protect them, usually with disruptive behavioural outcomes.[5]

As people who understand the greater value of sport and physical activity, not only in children, but throughout the whole of life, this is really upsetting.

Ironically it is often the children that do struggle behaviourally who thrive in an environment where sport is mentored well. It is equally interesting that children and adults alike who struggle with poor mental health are encouraged into the sport or physical activity arena.

At ***Be Skilled Be Fit*** we pride ourselves on delivering high quality professional sports education that encourages participation in a way that students can experience personal success, gaining confidence to participate in sport in other arenas.

---

[5] Miller, C. (27 February 2017). How Anxiety Leaders to Disruptive Behavior. The Sensory Spectrum. www.thesensoryspectrum.com/anxiety-leads-disruptive-behavior/.

"When sport isn't done well it can have a profoundly detrimental effect on children."

CHAPTER THREE

WINNING IS ABOUT MORE THAN MEDALS

One story that highlights the concept of 'winning is about more than medals' is about participation in the school athletics carnival. Athletics carnivals have existed through many generations and have always been an event that everyone looks forward to.

When we were at school, athletics carnivals were competitive. There was an expectation that everyone would participate. It was hard; it was fun. There were rivalries; there were positive, encouraging spectators, there were a few blisters from the tug of war. Records were broken, eggs were broken, and, quite possibly on occasion, a few ankles were broken in the three-legged race.

It was always a tiring and challenging day. It was always a day of wins and losses, toffee apples and a BBQ. It was ultimately a fun day for everyone, even for the teachers. Definitely more fun for some than others, but that was okay too.

Leanne remembers clearly one year she had the chicken pox, so she sat on the roof of her cubby that overlooked the schoolyard and didn't move for the entire day. She just needed to be a part of it somehow. She can still hear the buzz of 'noise' that loudly hummed throughout the entire day; it was such a happy sound. She had visitors all day long telling her of their wins, defeats, next events, and even throwing her a toffee apple! What a great day.

It doesn't feel like that these days; some students don't even go or participate in the events. Disappointingly some parents are on board with their children choosing to not participate or not attend their carnival. What has happened?

From our experience we see many students not wanting to participate in their athletics carnival due to poor skill development, low self-confidence and low self-esteem. This is a problem not because the athletics carnival is the be all and end all, but because the children are not emotionally or mentally willing to take the 'risk' of perhaps 'failing' in front of their peers, teachers, and parents.

A big part of this problem is that they don't feel like they have the basic skills required to simply participate in particular events.

One part of our job is to go into schools and teach athletics events prior to the carnival. Across many schools the result of doing this has resulted in a much greater participation rate of students at their school carnival. This alone is so exciting for us. On top of that, students from these schools are making it through to the Zone PSSA carnival when previously their school had no students qualifying for the Zone PSSA carnival.

What excites us is when the students that are willing to take a 'risk' and work with us to develop their technique realise that what they once saw as a 'failed' attempt was in fact a learning platform if they chose to actively learn from it.

We have also seen that prior to us coming in, some students have had little to no opportunity to learn how to even hold certain equipment, let alone use it correctly.

The experience of having a discus put in a student's hand, being talked through how to hold it, and how to throw it correctly changes their confidence so dramatically that they are then willing to participate at their carnival.

The feedback we constantly receive from schools after completing our athletics program is that more students actively participate, and more students perform better at their school carnival. The participation rate is far higher as the students have learned how to perform the skills correctly. They know how to pick up and hold a discus, how to throw a shot put, how to approach the high jump, how to take off in long jump. They are not scared of it anymore and feel more confident within themselves to be able to perform the skill without failure or looking silly.

This happens time and time again but on one occasion one boy, 'Tom', really stood out. Tom was not going to make the high jump finals or make it through to the Zone PSSA carnival, but that wasn't really his focus.

We were at his school running an athletics program in preparation for the school's athletics carnival. We were focusing on high jump, a little bit challenging and definitely a little scary if you aren't sure of what you're doing. Tom was willingly participating in this learning process but was neither confident nor comfortable with high jump.

On his first attempt to navigate his way over the intimidating bar before him he didn't make it over. He hit the bar, the bar fell, and he walked away head down to the end of the line not excited for his next jump. Some students made the jump and others didn't, there was no problem with that. It's what happened next that made all the difference.

It was obvious that Tom's demeanour had changed and there was a sense that he would really rather be doing anything else but high jump. As his turn was approaching again, he was told a couple of small but key things to change in his technique. He wasn't taking off with the correct foot or close enough to the mat and it was this he needed to focus on, not the fear of failing.

Taking the advice on board he said "okay, I will give it go," When his turn arrived, he executed what was discussed and he got over the bar for the first time that day. With that change of focus, positive feedback and encouragement he got over the jump and joined the end of the queue with his chest puffed out and was championed for his great achievement.

It was important for him in that moment that his classmates recognised his achievement also. He was obviously a well-liked boy, but not one of the 'cool kids', so for his classmates to hear the coaches say "wow, Tom you did it, awesome effort", that in turn evoked high-fives with his classmates who saw his great personal achievement in this moment. It is important to teach students how to be in each other's corner and that it does not take away from your own achievement by championing somebody else's achievement.

That feedback totally changed his attitude, and he was then keen for his next turn. He was happy to be there and had a much happier demeanour. While he waited for his next turn, we reinforced what we had previously told him and had a joke with him and a few others around him to encourage connection, encourage comradery and build rapport within his community. He was much more comfortable and ready to go for his next jump.

This particular sports class was so much bigger than just a great learning experience on a sports skill level. It was 'failure' turned into success, it was another opportunity to build connectivity and experience comradery, and it was an opportunity for peers to see that their support role is really important even when it feels small or insignificant to them. It was an opportunity for us to demonstrate that the 'gold medal' wins aren't always the most important wins in their day or in the day of their peers, friends, teammates, and others around them.

These teaching moments never stop and there are endless opportunities for learning, shaping and moulding in every lesson. However, we need to capitalise on these opportunities or vital life skill development will be missed. This is why we are so passionate about sport, especially in schools where we are in a protected environment. It's for this reason, with our twenty years of experience behind us, we send two sports educators per class group in order to achieve our aims for school sports classes.

Our aim of developing sports and skills in all of the students we teach simply can't be achieved to our standard in large groups.

In this instance, Tom not only learned basic high jump skills, but more importantly, perceived himself and his 'standing' in the group in a positive way. The experience encouraged him to go for more than what he believed he could do, and demonstrated that failure is only failure if you fail to improve, learn from it, and use it to propel you further.

It doesn't matter if you can high jump or not; that is totally irrelevant. It was the overall learning process that was important, and it was so encouraging to see Tom participate in high jump at the school athletics carnival. A great personal win for Tom.

CHAPTER FOUR

FEAR OF FAILURE

*"I've missed more than 9,000 shots in my career. I've lost almost 300 games. 26 times I've been trusted to take the game winning shot and missed. I've failed over and over again in my life.
That is why I SUCCEED."*

- MICHAEL JORDAN

It is nothing new that people generally don't like 'failure'. Of course we don't. It is hard not to see it as a negative result due to some sort of inadequacy. This makes it quite confronting and unpleasant to sit with.

If we were given the opportunity to embark on an opportunity in which we had no chance of failure, would we take it, and how long would we take to action it? Of course we would take it, and we would get started as soon as we could get our plan into action. It would be super exciting, and we don't think we would feel any sense of dread, negativity, or worry, just perhaps a little nervous, excited anticipation of the unknown of what we are embarking upon.

Why is this?

Research on fear of failure and procrastination has shown that students are being crippled and their academic growth stunted by an unhealthy and unmanaged fear of failure.

This is not just evidenced in Australia but worldwide, and it is not exclusive to school-aged children but across society.[6]

---

[6] Pychyl, T.A. Ph.D. (13 February 2009). Fear of Failure. Pyschology Today. www.psychologytoday.com/au/blog/dont-delay/200902/fear-failure.

As a parent, seeing children and younger generations not reaching their potential or failing to thrive in their moment to shine is hard to watch.

What are the stumbling blocks and how do we tackle them?

This is where it gets a bit messy. It's a case of what comes first: the chicken or the egg. It is one of life's certainties that we will fail. Interestingly we 'fail' as infants long before we even know what failure actually is. Ironically, we depend on failure or, more importantly, learnings from failure to grow and develop.

Just imagine if we as one-year-olds thought: "if I try and stand up take a step I could fall, so perhaps I might just stay sitting". We would never actually walk because it takes an active effort to enable us to walk or our muscles and balance won't develop. It wouldn't just suddenly happen at any age that it was attempted. It is the same for those incredibly inspiring people who walk again after debilitating accidents. It requires training and practice until you have the mental, emotional, physical, and behavioural skills required to conquer that challenge.

Seeing 'failure' as a negative result can translate into further feelings of mental, emotional, physical, behavioural, and social defeat. Ultimately, this way of thinking causes a backward step in growth. We should think of 'failure' as a stepping stone to moving forward. People who addressing the stumbling blocks to success and therefore win mentally, emotionally, physically, and socially will be propelled to future success.

Many people who experience negative results as failure will be very reluctant to risk trying because the social, emotional, and mental pain outweighs the need for success in the task.

Conversely, people who have a 'win' mentally, either socially or emotionally, will have a much bigger drive to attempt future challenges without a debilitating fear of failure.

This is such a complex area, and to try and put it in a nutshell is very difficult, but here it is. Those who feel emotionally and socially safe will feel more comfortable taking risks and pushing to, and through, failure more so than those who do not feel emotionally or socially safe.

It is important that we find strategies to address this present issue, as it is having a major impact on children and adults alike.

What can we expect if we don't find solutions?

- More underachievement
- A decrease in innovation
- Less participation
- Less intellectual growth
- Emotional instability
- Mental health issues
- Less diversity
- Less creativity
- Less ambition
- Limited experiences

We are seeing a concerning growth in young people with mental health challenges.[7]

---

[7] Fildes, C.E., Hall, J., Perrens, B., Perdriau, A., and Plummer, J. (2019) Youth Survey Report 2019. Mission Australia.

It is acknowledged that there is a rising problem of underachievement[8]. Suicide rates and self-harm in younger children is alarming.[9]

Disengagement, disconnection, and isolation is on the rise as 'socialisation' has shifted to the online platform of social media and the gaming world[10].

Our response to this has been to tread lightly; to back off and give them space, to take some of the pressures off them, allow them to learn in their own way and in their own time; to allow them greater choice, to have more voice in decision making and place less expectations on them.

Are these things helping them or are we just running scared of confronting them? Are we teaming up with this generation to do the hard yards to create a mentally, emotionally,

---

[8] (15 June 2018). Student stress on the rise – report. The Educator. www.theeducatoronline.com/k12/news/student-stress-on-the-rise--report/251165.

[9] Burton, M. (May 2019). Suicide and self-harm: vulnerable children and young people. Practice Nursing, 30. 10.12968/pnur.2019.30.5.218.

[10] White, R. (December 2015). The evolution of socialization. White Hutchison. www.whitehutchinson.com.

physically, socially, and well-functioning, happy generation who are ready and willing to thrive?

It is tough and it does feel scary, especially for those of us who are parents. Ironically in this chapter of 'fear of failure', a big factor for us is that we have the people most important to us at stake. This is an amazing life we have the benefit of experiencing, but for an alarming and growing number of people, including children as young as pre-schoolers, there is a very real, consuming and destructive dark side.

We need to get real with what is going wrong and be prepared to invest heavily in this generation of school children and do what it takes to get it right.

The importance of teamwork

It has to be a team effort and we all have our parts to play so that we can improve resilience and decrease the fear of failure.

Here are five practical ways that we have found work to make a difference in improving resilience against the fear of failure, utilising the sport platform:

✓ Develop a broad range of competencies

Studies have indicated that 'fear of failure', 'procrastination', and 'competencies' are all interconnected[11].

The more that children can gain in not just experience, but competency across a variety of skills, the more confident they will be in embarking on new experiences and striving for higher achievement within that.

It is important to highlight the word 'competency'. It is not simply 'having a go', it is shaping the skills involved to a competent level.

✓ Redefine 'failure' and 'success'

These two words: 'failure' and 'success', are quite black and white in children's eyes.

Practical demonstrations provide an opportunity to teach children that a failed attempt is simply finding the space for the next piece of

---

[11] Pychyl, T.A. Ph.D.. (13 February 2009). *Fear of Failure. Psychology Today.* https://www.psychologytoday.com/au/blog/dont-delay/200902/fear-failure.

refinement to then propel them to the next level. Sport is perfect platform for this. If children don't experience 'failure' they will not grow. The key here is we have to take responsibility for the coaching and mentoring role that goes with that. If a child fails without moving through it with correction and support and gaining growth, then yes, it is failure. If they are moved through their 'failures', or sticking points, then that is 'success'. That is their win in their moment right there. This is not a child's natural understanding of success and failure; we need to teach them this.

✓ 'Build' them up don't 'puff' them up

Society has moved towards 'giving a clap to fish for swimming'. Whilst praise is great, we need to be careful how we use it. As children grow older they know when they have worked hard or put effort in, had a good result, or shown improvement. Children equally know when they have not worked hard, put in any effort and didn't get the results that they were capable of achieving.

Let's respect them enough to be honest with them. If we are willing to say in partnership with them: "I thought you were capable of a better result than this, where do you think you went wrong?" and mentor them through it, that would be much more beneficial in building, developing, and growing them as a person. Instead we often take the easy route and say "good effort, better luck next time", or worse, "you did really well, there were just some really bad ref's calls."

This sounds harsh, but we need to avoid telling children how great they are just to give them a lift or 'puff' their ego. It does nothing to 'build' their character if it isn't genuinely warranted.

- ❖ Build their strengths
- ❖ Build their competencies
- ❖ Build their character
- ❖ Build their understanding
- ❖ Build their emotional stability
- ❖ Build their mental toughness
- ❖ Build their resilience
- ❖ Build their confidence
- ❖ Build stable foundations
- ❖ Build your relationship with them.

This will give them something solid to believe in themselves about.

✓ Emotionally / socially safe and positive environments

Again, *if done right*, the school sport platform presents a great opportunity for this to occur. If it is done wrong, it has the potential to do so much damage. Children are 'performing' in front of their peers constantly. In the classroom, at lunch, at recess, and in formal outdoor learning. The safer these environments and the more positive we can make these environments, the better the results not just in learning the given skill but in shaping the whole person within that.

✓ Be on their team

Let the students know that "I am on your team, and I want to help you 'win' today."

> *"Only those who dare to fail can ever achieve greatly"*
>
> ROBERT F. KENNEDY

CHAPTER FIVE

ACKNOWLEDGEMENT AND ATTENTION

A teenage boy comes out of school and declares to his mum and whoever is in earshot "mum, I did great today, I didn't get into any trouble!" His older sister very quickly pipes in with "well, fish don't get a clap for swimming."

Doesn't that hit the nail on the head?

We have all witnessed the two-year-old 'watch me' phase when they stand in front of you and say "watch me" and perform a jump for you. We say with enthusiasm "wow, great jump" so with that acknowledgement they declare "watch me" again to perform exactly the same jump, hoping for another resounding positive response. After about the fifth time you get the picture that they are actually quite proficient at this jump and really need to be shown another challenge that requires a bit more skill.

Maybe two jumps in a row or jumping over a line on the ground. The point being, let's keep requiring more of children within their capabilities. We are wired to want to please the people in our lives. This is both a good thing and a bad thing. Let's make sure we choose to be part of the 'good thing'. That means being trustworthy, invested, strong, positive role models who are capable of bringing the best out of them.

When our son was about the age of five, over a very short period of time, he developed quite a bad stutter. It quickly escalated to the point of needing speech therapy to address it. At that time, Leanne was a real straight-shooter. If something was not right, fix it. So, she was frustrated when she would say "stop stuttering" and that simply didn't change anything.

The speech therapist taught Leanne a lot. She had a very different method of treating the stuttering problem. As it happened, we would see her once a week to actually teach me what had to be done for the rest of the week. She was going to teach me how to achieve 'smooth talking' for our son.

Her program was very simple and very clear, but Leanne didn't have a great deal of confidence that this seemingly very basic concept would work.

Leanne had to give him ten praises before she could give him a correction on the 'bumpy words'. That was it, that was the program. Wow, this was basic but tough!

Firstly, this was just not how Leanne worked. Secondly, his stuttering at times was so bad that it was hard to find one praise let alone ten. Leanne literally had to ask him questions that he could answer in one word in the hope that it was a 'smooth word'. Thirdly Leanne was given the beginnings of a list of positive phrases of feedback that she had to give him on the occasions he had smooth talking. Phrases like "oooh, great smooth word" or "what a smooth sentence"; SO

NOT LEANNE! To be honest it felt condescending, but she did her best.

This little fish whom previously would not have got 'a clap for swimming' found himself out of water at this time, and needed those claps. So off we went, "great smooth talking," "that word was so smooth," "wow you said that long sentence smoothly," and so we went on ten times. Only then Leanne had one opportunity to say, "that word was a bit bumpy, let's try that again, wow that was a lot smoother," then back to ten more praises! Yes, it felt like a massive task that Leanne was just not sure about.

Well it worked! You wouldn't even know now that at one point our son had a significant stutter. Not only did his stutter completely disappear, but there was no residual negative social, emotional, mental, or behavioural impact on him at all. He just felt like therapy was 'play'.

From this experience we took a similar approach into our school sports programs. While we can't do ten praises to one correction, as there simply is not the time to achieve this, we still endeavor to fill the sport space with individual and group positive feedback as much as we can. We do this by using positive reinforcement of skills used in that lesson, then complimenting it with a further tweak of that skill to keep improvement happening.

For example, we might be doing jumps and landings off a mini trampoline. A student will jump and land in 'motor bike' and we might say "great motor bike arms, next jump look ahead at me and tell me how many fingers am I holding up." This helps them to keep their head up looking forward. Constant, small improvements along the way.

We see children thrive in this environment of 'progress not perfection', and we believe in giving them a constant present audience encouraging them to achieve.

Praise, reinforcement, challenge, growth

As kids get older the 'acknowledgment and attention' looks a little different. They don't need nor want us to give them a 'clap for swimming'. That teenage boy was not looking for a clap, he was just having a joke and it was funny. Children love an audience. They get to a point where they don't want to be clapped for something trivial, they want to be seen and respected and to feel like they matter and what they do matters.

Children love interactions with adults that they respect. Respect goes both ways; children need to respect their teachers, coaches, mentors, and parents and know that these adults respect them back. Often that is tricky, but we are the adults in this equation, so we need to set the tone and be willing to shape what respect looks like in good, healthy, positive relationships.

If we can earn their respect, rather than simply expect it, then we will have a more significant, positive impact on their overall growth and development than if we think we can just demand their respect due to authority.

Once we have their respect, they will have a positive, ready for growth mindset. They will want to team up with us.

If they are not getting the acknowledgement and attention they crave and need from good, strong, healthy, positive role models they will go searching for it somewhere else.

CHAPTER SIX

ENGAGEMENT AND CONNECTIVITY

Studies have shown that a lack of social connection is a far greater determinant of health than obesity, smoking or high blood pressure.[12]

While we knew that connectivity for people of all ages was very important, we had no idea that lack of connectivity presented such a severe health risk. For us, this is particularly alarming

---

[12] Sepällä, E. (23 March 2020). Social connection boosts health even when you're isolated. Emma Sepällä. emmaseppala.com/connect-thrive-infographic/.

as the 'disconnect', or 'sense of belonging' is increasing in school age children.[13]

Disconnection is affecting our health

Why is disconnect occurring?

- ❖ Social inadequacy
- ❖ Emotional insecurity
- ❖ Growing behavioural issues
- ❖ Fear of rejection
- ❖ Fear of judgment
- ❖ Hiding behind social media

It is increasingly important at the school age level that we actively teach children how to make and foster genuine, strong, healthy connections, and show them what genuine, strong, healthy connections look like. Not just with a few good friends in your 'group' but thinking broader.

If we are willing to see past our close group of friends and see the potential for friendships that may look a little unusual at first, we will

---

[13] Thomson, S. (June 2018). *Many Australian school students feel they 'don't belong' in school: new research.* The Conversation. theconversation.com/many-australian-school-students-feel-they-dont-belong-in-school-new-research-97866.

most likely find many connection points with many people around us that we may not have seen before.

For example, our daughter, the 'sporty girl' now asks to get to school early so that she can play handball with the self-proclaimed 'nerd group'.

We loved hearing this for a few reasons:

1. She has found value in her brief moment of time with this group.
2. They value her for the fun they have with her before school.
3. They are chatting within the group to get to know each other on different levels for each of them.
4. They all now have another 'connection point'; it enlarges their spheres of connection.
5. They learn a newfound respect for each other due to learning more about each other.
6. They may not have a lot in common, but they share more than expected.
7. They are all now that bit more comfortable in their environment with a broader range of 'belonging'.

8. It has opened an opportunity for others as they arrive at school to also become involved with their morning handball ritual, which contributes to an extended 'friendship group' experience. We love this!

You don't need to be everyone's best friend

Not everyone needs to be your best friend, and you don't need to be everyone's best friend.

How great though, if we could build a community for ourselves made up of layers of friendships that are:
- ❖ Diverse
- ❖ Interesting
- ❖ Supportive
- ❖ Encouraging
- ❖ Positive
- ❖ Enlightening
- ❖ Engaging
- ❖ Fun
- ❖ Tangible
- ❖ Fulfilling
- ❖ Interactive
- ❖ Challenging
- ❖ Generational

We think we would all look at that list and be willing to say that we need a pretty diverse and layered community around us to tick all of those boxes. That's what healthy community living is about, and it is achievable.

You realise as an adult that in a situation where you are surrounded by people you don't know, you find great comfort in the person across the room who you do know. You may not have considered them a friend as such, but the familiarity is of great comfort.

Talking about what friendship looks like has brought to mind a gorgeous book our daughter has, called *Unlikely Friendships*, by Jennifer S. Holland. Jennifer is a science researcher, which has led her to see first-hand many unlikely friendships in the animal world. Friendships such as a dog and a piglet, a hippo and a goat, a dear and a dog, an iguana and a cat, and many more. These are true stories of long-term relationships and bonds between these unlikely friends. What rich friendships might we be missing out on if we don't open ourselves up to our own 'unlikely friendships'?

Looking at this list and perhaps looking at some friends we have in our own lives, most of us can probably relate in our own diverse friendship group to what some of these unlikely friendships look like. There are some pretty obscure friends in our community, that's for sure, and we are so grateful for that!

Community has to be modelled, purposefully taught, and fostered in children or they will not understand its significance and importance, and they will not know how to achieve it. If they can understand this, then create and develop this for themselves as children, they will take the same concept as well as many of the same friends through life. In our experience, we need community more and more as we get older.

If we can instil this in children at a young age and help enable this to start taking place in their lives while they are young, then as life throws curveballs they will have a community ready to support them through it. Not only does it create a safety net or support group when things get tough, community also helps us to see that we are important to others and that they need what we have to offer. It is important for children and adults to know and feel like they are wanted and needed in the lives of their peers and their community. It becomes a safe place in which we feel like we belong.

'Community' used to happen somewhat naturally when neighbourhood living looked a little different than it does today. For several reasons it doesn't just take shape naturally, so we need to be intentional about it and intentional in teaching children how to find it in their lives.

Community

Community is a living breathing force in our lives, and it needs to be attended to, for it to grow.

As sports educators, mentors, and teachers we can see the huge potential for community and connectedness to flourish in the realm of sport. 'In school' sport is the perfect place to implement strategies to bring the concept of community to life. It is also a great stepping-stone to develop the skills and experiences required to feel confident about participating in out-of-school sport in a more formal arena.

If the groundwork is done at the school level to develop the emotional, social, mental, and physical skills required to enable a child to embark on sport outside of school, then it will serve as an endless investment into growing their community. It is disappointing that it is only a small number of people who continue to include sport in their life once they have left school. We believe that a part of the reason for this is because they don't feel confident or equipped to feel safe in the sport environment. We can change this at the school level if we implement sport well and intentionally.

Sport brings people and groups together. It's a real opportunity for schools to utilise sport to its full potential. Sport is a platform for schools to have an impact on engagement and connectivity in a positive way outside of the classroom experience.

It's great experience for us to have had the opportunity to work with teachers in team-building or bonding sessions. It is quite challenging presenting a sports-focussed team-building activity to teachers for a few reasons.

As we prepare their team-building experience, these are the voices we hear:

- ❖ I don't do sport; I don't even have sport shoes!
- ❖ Will we have to run?
- ❖ I don't want to get sweaty!
- ❖ Do we have to do it if it rains?
- ❖ Do we have to do it if it's hot?
- ❖ Do we have to do it?
- ❖ Is it going to be competitive?
- ❖ I don't want to do the team thing!
- ❖ I can't do it!
- ❖ I'm going to look stupid!

Does this all sound fairly accurate? In our experience, we and the teachers always have a great time in these exercises. They usually take the form of an 'Amazing Race' style of event. We consider the group and understand that it is necessary to be mindful and respectful of the varying dynamics of the group.

Having said that, the participants usually find themselves really enjoying participating in activities that they either have not done before, or activities they would not usually get involved in. They are also having fun and being challenged within a group of people they may not necessarily consider 'friends' as such.

- ❖ It creates a new connection point, perhaps just a small one but they are all significant.
- ❖ They have the opportunity to experience a different side of each other. It could be good, it could be bad; it all counts.
- ❖ It extends them out of their comfort zone; even just the anticipation of not knowing what will be required of them.
- ❖ They realise after the fact that they were okay, they survived it.
- ❖ They probably laughed together.
- ❖ They probably found out something new about their work colleagues/teammates.
- ❖ They possibly found out something new about themselves.
- ❖ They were energised by it.

From that small experience so much happens. It's the small things, like the points listed above, that create who we are as people and where and how we fit into our community. This is our philosophy when we work with children in sport. It's the small things in their time with us that amount to contributing and shaping who they are as people.

Sport is much more than just games

Teach children about circles of connectedness

If we can teach children the concept of having layers of connection then they can see more clearly where and how different people can fit into their lives.

- ❖ **INNER CORE** - You will have your closest, most trusted friends. These could be family, or a small number of people you know very well, and they know you very well, and you have mutual trust. Finding these people is a learning process that we have all experienced. You may not interact with these people daily, but you know they aren't going anywhere. These relationships take a while to form and they are usually in your life over a long period of time.

- ❖ **OUTER CORE** – These tend to be people who you 'hang with'; they tick a lot of boxes, they add value to our lives. We are comfortable with them. We can be ourselves around them without fear of judgment and we tend to have a lot of common ground and enjoy the similar way we do life. There is openness within this group and a tight bond. They tend to know a lot about us and we are okay with that. Sometimes this is simply born from spending a lot of time with them. For example as part of a school group, or as particular people within that school group.

❖ **THE EXTENSIONS** – For children, school takes up the bulk of their time, but after that comes the extensions of who they are. For example, afternoon activities such as sport, music, dance, study group, book club, and other interest groups. These will most likely be a group of friends that are specifically connected due to a common interest. These friendships grow through participation in challenges, fun, and competition, and through the shared camaraderie within that experience. This layer is quite varied due to the time spent with these groups of people, the age group, and the level of intensity of what they are doing, along with potential concerts, travel, or extended periods of time and commitment to specific causes or competitions that they may be involved in together. All of these things, and more, bring groups and individuals within these groups closer. Whilst a connection point is made with the whole group on some level, bigger connection points are made with specific individuals.

- ❖ **THE ONLINE DIMENSION** – This is potentially one that can be really difficult to navigate and be very confusing and challenging for children (and adults). So many factors come into this; it really has its own circles of connectedness. What makes this much more difficult and dangerous to navigate is that you are often doing it 'blind'. There are a lot more unknowns to be navigated and it can be a very dangerous space. It is, however, still a space for children to have another dimension to their friendship groups and extend their sense of belonging, and it can be a positive part of their circles of connectedness if managed well. Navigating these friendships and acquaintances is even more difficult to begin with as children don't have a well-developed radar.

If we take the school community as an isolated example of being particularly large 'circles of connectedness' on its own, we can see how we as teachers, mentors and coaches can facilitate and encourage children to start broadening, understanding, and appreciating their circles of friendships.

Being raised in a sports-driven family, David can see and appreciate how sport filled his circles of connectedness even just at the school level.

You may have only spoken to some of these people in one sport session a week, but within that you develop a connection with someone that you may have never otherwise crossed paths with or thought that you had anything in common with. These moments are perfect for opening up new connection points.

It is hard for those who always just 'fit in' to understand the destructive nature of isolation; the sense of not belonging or not 'fitting in'. It is a very uncomfortable place to sit and it causes a lot of pain and social and emotional discomfort to an alarming and growing number of children.[14]

Imagine if every child in every school could walk into their school environment and know

---

[14] Allen, Dr K-A., Kern, Dr P., Waters, Prof L., Vella-Brodrick, Prof D. (15 July 2018). Why don't australian school kids feel a sense of belonging? The University of Melbourne. pursuit.unimelb.edu.au/articles/why-don-t-australian-school-kids-feel-a-sense-of-belonging.amp

that they had a comfortable place to sit within their school community. We feel that by utilising the school sport platform we can assist in bringing unlikely friendships together and inadvertently help children build an environment where they feel more comfortable to be themselves and to be accepted.

By being more conscious of our circles of connectedness we can become better at knowing where people sit in our lives. It is really important for children in particular to become more aware of the different layers of where their friends might sit. This has become more important in the 'likes generation' as there is such a shift to building a massive connection base as opposed to establishing more tangible 'connectedness'.

In *Be Skilled Be Fit* programs we endeavour to encourage a group or team environment where all particpants can be recognised and encouraged by each other in positive interactions.

CHAPTER SEVEN

WHAT TO LOOK FOR IN YOUR SPORTS PROVIDER

✓ **Small groups**

Two sports educators per class group is essential if you are serious about seeing actual skill development in the students at your school. That way the class can be split into smaller groups to ensure actual skill development and that educators have more to work with students on the life skills mentioned previously. As we keep talking about, there is far more to impart on students than just sport skills. Small groups allow for more focused attention on each student and gives them the opportunity to feel like they are being watched and that their achievements are being noticed.

Children thrive on this attention and we find that we get more from them when they see us watching them 'perform'. Two staff per class also means that there is less waiting time for a child's turn. It also allows students to be treated as individuals and for us to specifically tailor the program rather than use a 'group mentality'. Small groups require less 'crowd management' as they are always engaged and therefore they are more conducive to mentoring opportunities.

Teachers would agree that smaller class sizes would result in greater productivity and effectiveness in teaching, which is exactly what we offer.

✓ Experience counts

It is not as easy as it looks. It is important that providers have the experience and the knowledge to create a program that incorporates a wide and varying range of sport competencies. It is important that these programs can be adapted for different areas and schools, and on the spot for differing skill levels within any class group. The programs need to incorporate stages of development appropriately. Individual staff need to have the skills required to coach the students through the delivery of that program in a professional and safe manner with the specific knowledge of how to correct technique and manage a class group effectively.

Many times we have heard that promises have simply not been kept, to the detriment of the student's development.

✓ Bigger Picture Focus

If you are trying to adopt our vision of sport, encompassing so much more than sport skills alone, then your provider needs to specifically have that vision as well.

As we mentioned earlier in the book, if the social, emotional, mental and behavioural aspects aren't addressed intentionally, they will be poorly shaped with quite possibly a detrimental effect. If the sports provider doesn't specifically train their staff in 'positive mentoring' and the 'bigger picture' focus, then they will be lacking consistency and continuity across staff.

We feel that if the 'bigger picture' mindset is not specifically one of their major focus points then it is probably not part of their staff development program.

Most sports providers are purely focused on getting children more active and churning large numbers through a program to simply tick a box.

We find the 'bigger picture' mindset comes with years of experience working with all ages of children over a long period of time, gaining the insight and understanding of how sport plays a vital role in shaping children.

✓ Quality technical feedback

Quality feedback is very important in any teaching process and there are a few steps involved in that process for it to be effective. We have to be able to see where positive changes can be made.

It can be particularly difficult in sport to isolate where technique is not quite right. It is not like maths, for example, where if they show the 'working', it pinpoints where they are going wrong; sport and sport competencies happen at speed.

To use a very basic example of throwing a tennis ball at a target, there are key points to the action required for a positive and correct result. To start with, the coach needs to know the skill breakdown across all the competencies they are teaching for all ages. Then, as the students throw a ball in that split second, we need to be able to identify where their action needs tweaking to attain a better result in their next throw. If this doesn't happen then, not only are they practicing the wrong technique, they are not hitting the target they are aiming for so they are getting frustrated and feeling like they can't do it. This situation is frustrating for us as it would usually only take a small correction to achieve a good result and completely change that experience for the student.

In our experience, constant feedback goes a long way; small comments to every student. For example, if they are throwing a ball into a bucket you could verbalise the good technique that you are seeing: "great high elbow", "nice high pointing arm", 'I can see your eyes on the target", then add what they are missing: "turn your foot to point to your target" etc. These comments along the way let them know they are being watched and that we are wanting them to succeed at this skill.

We find that if we are invested in what they are doing then students will be too.

✓ The lesson and the staff

The staff who visit your school need to be trained and invested in the bigger picture of the company they represent. They need to be fully prepared with lesson plans and extensive quality gear that allows the students to have as much hands-on experience as possible. They need to have a structured lesson plan that is stage appropriate; that involves learning tasks and the specific skills being taught, then adequate time to practice the skill with as much positive feedback as possible.

Staff need to be enthusiastic, engaged, invested, verbal, fun and positive role models.

If you have any further questions regarding school Personal Development, Health and Physical Education programs, please contact us at ***Be Skilled Be Fit*** and we would be very happy to assist.

CHAPTER EIGHT

OUR STORY

We both have a very similar background story. We were both raised in a family environment that embraced the value of sport. Interestingly, Leanne's mother was not raised in sport but knew how much she had missed out on and made it an important part of her plan for raising her own children. She could see how it would make her kids tough, strong, disciplined, committed, focused, and busy! Leanne has two sisters and one brother and they were all involved in sport from a very young age, and all still value sport and fitness in their lives.

We can both see very clearly how sport has

shaped who we are today on so many levels and appreciate the benefits of that. It was only recently, a teammate from Leanne's younger netball days posted on Facebook that she would love to be playing netball again with the girls in this team. So many of those girls, including Leanne, replied to that post acknowledging how great it was and what great friendships were made. This was over twenty years ago and these ladies are still talking about it today.

This is just one thing that the richness of sport brings to our lives; the connections we make along the way with our fellow teammates and competitors, potentially from all over the country and even across the world.

We would both say now that one of the really great parts of our parenting is that we have both come to the point of being able to play a sport in the same teams as our children, now that they are nearing adulthood themselves. Having this experience is definitely a highlight.

After various jobs and studies we started as personal trainers and, whilst doing that, increasingly we were asked to train our clients' children, as they were sedentary and becoming overweight. This was confronting and sad for us as while working with this growing number of children, we could see that they didn't feel like they had the skills to play sports and would have been embarrassed at even giving it a try.

We could see that they lacked confidence in themselves and didn't know how they could become a part of the different sports avenues, even at the school level. We also felt that being personal trainers to children helped them, it didn't quite seem to be exactly what they needed from us. We began sports fundamentals programs for school children and this way we could incorporate sports skills, fitness, friendships, and fun. This seemed a much better fit for us and something that addressed the root of many issues.

With the increasing number of children attending our programs, and the realisation that basic sports skills and confidence were not great, we knew that this opportunity needed to be offered to as many children as we could reach. We collaborated and developed programs based around the school curriculum to address this growing problem.

After almost twenty years of providing wide-ranging sport programs including fundamental movement skills, gymnastics, athletics, and sport-specific programs under the ***Be Skilled Be Fit*** banner we have learned so much. We now understand a much bigger picture of the impact that sport, done well, has on creating a brighter future for children. We have become passionate about utilising the in-school sport platform to build character, confidence, mental, physical, social, and emotional well-being, and building broader friendship connection points to help reduce issues such as behavioural problems, anxiety, fear of failure, obesity, isolation, and poor self-esteem. We have seen over and over again how good sports programs that take the 'bigger picture' approach can impact all of these areas.

This has been our story so far. We hope that the next part of our story involves supporting a more confident, competent, and emotionally strong generation to thrive, excel, and achieve. It is a great pleasure to be a part of so many children's' lives. We have seen, for us, that the older we get, the more we say that raising socially, mentally, emotionally, and physically healthy children is very much a team effort. We are so excited that the part we play in that is in the space of 'fun'. We are very aware that within that 'fun', these things need to remain at the forefront so they can be constantly addressed intentionally.

This is our focus and our passion.

CHAPTER 9

HOW TO CONTACT US

If you would like assistance in developing the Personal Development, Health and Physical Education Programs at your school, please contact us to discuss how we can help.

beskilledbefit.com.au
office@beskilledbefit.biz
+ 61 2 4774 0338

www.ingramcontent.com/pod-product-compliance
Lightning Source LLC
Chambersburg PA
CBHW030456010526
44118CB00011B/961